"Steichen is first of all interested in life . . . a scientist and a speculative philosopher stands back of Steichen's best pictures. They will not yield their meaning and essence on the first look nor the thousandth—which is the test of masterpieces. . . . He will die telling God that if he could live a few years longer he might be the photographer he wanted to be. . . . He will die a seeker and a listener."

Carl Sandburg, STEICHEN: THE PHOTOGRAPHER

"It was not by accident or as a stunt that Carl, a poet, was invited to speak before a joint session of Congress on a Lincoln's Birthday. Carl has often zig-zagged back and forth across the United States, speaking and reading his poems, reaching the hearts as well as the minds of millions of young Americans. I believe 'The People, Yes' is his finest poem, a major work ringing forth as an authentic voice of the 'American Dream' and it establishes Carl Sandburg as an integral part of the American earth."

Edward Steichen, 1966

Sandburg

"I am credulous about the destiny of man,
and I believe more than I can ever prove
of the future of the human race
and the importance of illusions,
the value of great expectations.
I would like to be in the same moment
an earthworm (which I am) and
a rider to the moon (which I am)."

THE PEOPLE, YES

SANDBURG

Photographers View Carl Sandburg

Edited and with an Introduction by Edward Steichen

Harcourt, Brace & World, Inc.
New York

To the photographers who made this book possible

The quotations from Carl Sandburg's works are reprinted by permission of Harcourt, Brace & World, Inc. and of Holt, Rinehart and Winston, Inc. They are from: *Smoke and Steel; Selected Poems*, edited by Rebecca West; *Honey and Salt; Harvest Poems; Good Morning, America; The People, Yes; Complete Poems; Abraham Lincoln: The War Years; Always the Young Strangers; The American Songbag; Rootabaga Stories*, copyright © 1920, 1922, 1926, 1927, 1936, 1960 by Harcourt, Brace & World, Inc.; copyright © 1928, 1948, 1950, 1952, 1953, 1955, 1956, 1963, 1964 by Carl Sandburg; *Cornhuskers*, copyright 1918 by Holt, Rinehart and Winston, Inc., copyright 1946 by Carl Sandburg; *Chicago Poems*, copyright 1916 by Holt, Rinehart and Winston, Inc., copyright 1944 by Carl Sandburg. The pictures on pages 38, 104 (bottom), 109, and 112 by John Vachon are from *Look* Magazine, copyright © 1956, Cowles Communications, Inc.; the color insert, by J. Baylor Roberts, following page 68 is © National Geographic Society; pages 94 and 95 are © Arnold Newman.

First edition

Library of Congress Catalog Card Number: 65-19070

Printed in the United States of America by Davis, Delaney, Inc.

Book design by Kathleen Haven

Photographers

Alexander Alland, 25
Leonard H. Bass, 89
Kay Bell, 36, 37
Robert Buchbinder, 46 (bottom), 92 (middle)
Harry M. Callahan, 58 (top), 98
Harvey Croze, 100
Herbert Dallinger, 63 (top)
Myron H. Davis, 58 (bottom), 59
Nell Dorr, 8, 29
Garrison, 32
June Glenn, Jr., 35, 52, 85, 96, 97, 107, 110
Allan Gould, 48, 49 (bottom)
Hans Hammarskiold, 71, 78, 79, 80, 81, 82, 83, 84 (top and middle)
Declan Haun, 108 (bottom)
Lionel Heymann, 64 (top right, bottom left, bottom right)
Frederic B. Knoop, 34 (top left and right), 39, 42, 53 (top), 108 (top)
Robert L. Knudsen, 103
R. Ned Landon, 64 (top left)

Archie Lieberman, 93
Margrethe Mather, 10
Dan McCoy, 50, 104 (top), 106 (bottom), 113
John McKinney, 105
Herbert Mitgang, 54, 70, 72, 73, 74, 106 (top)
Arnold Newman, 94, 95
J. Baylor Roberts, color insert following 68
James B. Rutledge, 61
Eric Schaal, 33
I. W. Schmidt, 53 (bottom), 92 (top)
Gerald Smith, 90 (top right)
William A. Smith, 43 (bottom), 47, 101
Dana Steichen, ii, iii, 20, 21, 22, 23, 24, 31, 34 (bottom)
Edward Steichen, 1, 11, 12, 14, 15 (top right), 16, 17, 18, 19, 26, 27, 30, 43 (top), 44, 45, 49 (top), 51, 55, 56, 57
Harry L. Taylor, 6
John Vachon, 38, 104 (bottom), 109, 112
Thomas E. Walters, 84 (bottom), 111
Edward Weston, 10
John R. Whiting, 41 (bottom)

Sources of Photographs

Chicago *Daily News*, 46 (top)
Columbia Broadcasting System, 90 (top left)
Parade (Allan Gould), 48, 49 (bottom)
Keystone View Company, 13
Lawrence-Phillip Studios, 63 (bottom)
The Library of Congress, 60
Collection of Museum of Modern Art, 1, 10, 56, 57

The Progressive Farmer (John McKinney), 105
Metro News Photos, 76 (top)
National Broadcasting Company, 90 (top right)
George Stevens' "The Greatest Story Ever Told," 91
Milwaukee *Sentinel*, 6
The White House, 99, 102
Wide World Photos, Inc., 41 (top), 69, 86 (bottom)

We have made every effort to identify the photographers who took the pictures in this book. If anyone has information about any photographer who has not been identified, we will be glad to list him in the next edition.

In 1907, I was visiting my father and mother at their farm at Menomonee Falls, Wisconsin, some twenty miles from Milwaukee when my little sister, Lillian, turned up and announced that a man was coming to see her the next day—a poet—and she was interested in him. Well that threw my mother into a real dither. Nothing like that had ever occurred to her. Lillian was still her little girl. This was serious.

Then there was considerable discussion about what should be prepared for dinner the next day. Nearly every suggestion that my little sister made, my mother turned down. We came to chicken—no that wouldn't do. She said that poets when they did eat wanted something substantial and a lot of it, so they settled on turkey.

The next morning, my sister drove off with our horse and buggy to the Menomonee Falls station to pick up this fellow, Carl. Now she had told us that he was a poet. That's about all anybody knew about him at the time, that he had said he was a poet. This was almost a decade before *Chicago Poems* was published.

My mother was quite excited about his visit, but my father was very glum. I would see him go to the window and look out across the fields, and could hear him think, "My god, another longhair. He'll never be able to be any help on this farm."

Finally, Carl and my sister drove up. Carl was gallant. It wasn't raining, so he didn't have to put his mantle on the ground for her to step on, but he did lift her down.

My mother welcomed him with enthusiasm. She told my sister, "What a wonderful thing to have another artist in this family."

My father said, "How do you do."

And then Carl and I took a little walk outside, and when we came back, the turkey my mother had decided on was in the oven, and those two girls, Mother and Lillian, were going to that oven every two or three minutes to baste the turkey. It was surely the champion of basted turkeys in the world.

The oven was never really closed for more than a minute at a time. How the turkey finally got roasted I will never understand.

A month or two later, there was a marriage. My sister acquired a husband; I acquired a brother; and Lillian acquired a new name—Paula.

Probably the thing that Carl's final literary reputation will rest on is the fact that he wrote the first biography of a living photographer.

Of course, he also wrote a good one of Abraham Lincoln!

We saw lots of each other over the ensuing years when I went out to visit my parents, who were living in Elmhurst, Michigan, where Carl and Lillian made their home. I saw the kids—first Margaret, and then Helga and Janet—come into the world and grow up. I remember long walks Carl and I would take of an evening, after the kids were in bed, and we would go out into the country. Four or five blocks out of Elmhurst, and you were in the corn belt. We would walk for hours and hours through the night from village to village along the roads and the railroad track that sometimes ran straight through a cornfield. We heard the corn grow, and in our talk we straightened out the world a little. But I don't know whether there has been much change, yet.

Sometimes we would stop for a bag of popcorn and sometimes for a glass of beer, depending on which we could get. We both preferred the beer, but we settled for popcorn when there was no beer around.

It drew us close together. We got to know each other's dreams and aspirations and we have remained that way ever since.

I remember writing to Carl when he and Paula were still living in Michigan that we would make real progress in the arts in America only when the various artists in the different arts learned to collaborate on a project together. That didn't quite happen, but at least Carl and I worked together a couple of times—first, when my exhibition "Road to Victory," for which he wrote the captions, was displayed during the Second World War, and then later, when he wrote the magnificent preface to my book, *The Family of Man*.

Taking liberties with the last lines of a poem by James Whitcomb Riley, the Hoosier poet, I'd like to say, "When God made Carl, he didn't do nothing else that day but just sit around and feel good."

The pages of this book, reproducing the work of many photographers, famous and little-known, can be considered as both a collective visualization of Carl and a tribute to him as a citizen and poet by the photographers.

Carl's incisive gift for seeing and perceiving the essence of people, places, and things American is familiar to anyone who has read his books. The personal whims and predilections of his everyday living are not so well known, except to his more intimate friends.

For instance, he likes coffee, and he likes to smoke, but he is anything but an epicure about either. As long as it is coffee, whether it is tired or fresh, whether it is made from the best beans or just any old beans, it is all the same to him, and he refers to it as "the Java." When he traveled he always carried a can of instant coffee which he mixed with the warm water running from the hotel faucet. If he had a cup from a lunch wagon, it satisfied and fortified him.

He is a cigar smoker, but there again, any cigar is a good cigar. When he gets a cigar, whether by purchase or from a host, he cuts it in half, puts one half in his pocket and lights the other half. This is probably a hangover from his early days when he smoked Pittsburgh Stogies, a long cigar, tightly wrapped. When smoked, a Pittsburgh Stogie emitted an odor that made it smell as if it had been dipped in tar. Ordinarily a cigar smoker will discard the cigar when it has been smoked down to an inch and a half or two inches, but not Carl. He smokes it to the bitter end, and when it gets so short he can no longer hold it, he sticks into it his penknife, which then serves as a holder.

Because Carl knew poverty and hunger in his early days, he considers tobacco and food as something to be consumed, and not wasted. I am sure he has unintentionally complimented the cooking of many a hostess by eating every last vestige of food on his plate.

He is a night owl as far as his writing hours are concerned, and consequently is a very late sleeper. At home, his daughter Janet puts his breakfast on a tray and coffee in a Thermos bottle, and places it in front of his door around eight in the morning. He wakes up at this hour, finds his breakfast outside his door, eats it, and then goes back to sleep again. He puts in an appearance at lunchtime, and after lunch, as well as after dinner, takes a walk. When he was younger these walks were usually long and vigorous. Gradually, they have become shorter and shorter.

He enjoys a glass of beer or a glass of wine, but will drink the latter from the bottom of a bottle of any old wine that has been opened for a week with as much enjoyment as he will take a glass from a freshly opened bottle of a rare old vintage.

He enjoys good intellectual conversation, but seems equally to enjoy the prattle of small children; he relishes a serious conversation with his peers as well as the maudlin and muddled opinions of the town drunk.

He is not a person of easy prejudices, but when an occasional one does develop, he has a loyalty to it. For many years he would not let anyone photograph him wearing glasses. Finally I told him that when a person who constantly wears glasses removes them for a picture, his eyes do not focus correctly. Then at last Carl changed his practice.

When Carl walks outdoors at Connemara he wears a peaked cap. When the weather is hot he wears an eyeshade to protect his eyes from the sun or the glare from the clouds or an open sky.

Some time ago, he always wore a kerchief loosely tied around his neck. When I chided him about this he said it was to protect his throat, but I believe it was more to have the feeling of pleasure in participating in the customs of another period. One time he carried a small shawl over his shoulders, and at another period he wrapped it over his knees when he sat down.

In many people these things might easily be considered affectations. In Carl they were part and parcel of his method of immersing himself, physically as well as mentally, in the period and personalities he was studying and writing about. Affectation is as far from being a part of Carl as is crime. All the important matters of his heart and mind stand revealed in his writings.

EDWARD STEICHEN

"There is a touch of two hands that foils all dictionaries. . . ."
GOOD MORNING, AMERICA

"Mr. and Mrs."
Carl Sandburg with his wife, Lillian Steichen Sandburg, Elmhurst, Illinois, 1923

(Left) *Clara Mathilda Anderson. My mother "had fair hair, between blond and brown—the color of oat straw just before the sun tans it—eyes light-blue, the skin white as fresh linen by candlelight, the mouth for smiling. She had ten smiles for us to one from our father."*

(Right) *August Sandburg. "My father was a 'black Swede,' his hair straight and black, his eyes black with a hint of brown, eyes rather deep-set in the bone, and the skin crinkled with his smile or laugh. . . . His hands thick with calluses, he was strictly 'a horny-handed son of toil.'"*

ALWAYS THE YOUNG STRANGERS

(Opposite) *At fifteen in 1893: "It came over me often that I wasn't getting anywhere in particular. . . . I heard that the Union Hotel barbershop wanted a porter. I said, 'Barbering is a trade. . . .' I hired to Mr. Humphrey at three dollars a week, shoeshine money, and tips. . . . Spring came after fall and winter months in the barbershop and doubts had been growing in me that I wasn't cut out for a barber."*

ALWAYS THE YOUNG STRANGERS

(Above) *"I was thirteen years of age when, with seven other boys, I took the sacrament and was confirmed as a member of the Elim Lutheran Church,"* Galesburg, Illinois. *(Carl Sandburg is on the left in the front row.)*

ALWAYS THE YOUNG STRANGERS

(Below) *"One Sunday afternoon a bunch of us had come together in front of the Olson store, most of us about sixteen or seventeen years of age. We were going to have a photograph made of the bunch. We counted and there were twelve of us. Someone said, 'Then we can show people what the Dirty Dozen looks like.' And the name Dirty Dozen stuck."* *(Carl Sandburg is on the right in the top row.)*

ALWAYS THE YOUNG STRANGERS

After receiving an honorable discharge as a member of Company C, Sixth Infantry Regiment of Illinois Volunteers, during the Spanish-American War, Sandburg returned to Galesburg, where he found a job as a "call man" in the fire department at ten dollars a month, and enrolled in Lombard College.

"I enrolled at Lombard for classes in Latin, English, inorganic chemistry, and elocution, drama, and public speaking. . . . I had to leave class when the fire whistle blew but that wasn't often enough to bother either the class or the professor. I was going to get an education."

ALWAYS THE YOUNG STRANGERS

(Top) Newspaperman Carl Sandburg and his wife join some of his journalist colleagues in entertaining Daniel V. Hoan, City Attorney of Milwaukee, at the home of Chester M. Wright in West Allis, Wisconsin. (Back) C. L. Dennis, Daniel V. Hoan, Carl Sandburg, Harry L. Wilbur, Chester M. Wright. (Front) Mrs. Dennis, Mrs. Harry L. Taylor, Mrs. Sandburg, Mrs. Wilbur, Mrs. Wright.

(Bottom) Sandburg later served as secretary to Emil Seidel during his term as Socialist Mayor of Milwaukee.

With a classmate at Lombard, Fred Dickinson, Sandburg helped to pay his college expenses by selling stereopticon slides for $2.00 a dozen.

"A lone gray bird,
   Dim-dipping, far-flying,
   Alone in the shadows and grandeurs and tumults
   Of night and the sea
   And the stars and storms."

Carl and Paula Sandburg with their daughters, Helga, Janet, and Margaret at the edge of
the sandblow near their home in Michigan in 1930

With Dan and Cully, his Irish setters, at home at Chikaming Farm, Michigan

Helga and Janet Sandburg with their father at Elmhurst, Illinois, in 1921

(Top left) Carl and Margaret Sandburg entertain Eugene V. Debs at their home in Elmhurst, Illinois.

(Bottom left) Carl and his mother join Helga and Janet on the swing in the yard of the Elmhurst house.

(Top right) Helga, Janet, and Margaret with their parents in Michigan

(Bottom right) Carl Sandburg and his daughter Margaret at their Hermitage Avenue home in Chicago

Carl Sandburg regards Carl Sandburg, a clear bright sky-blue delphinium named after him by its originator, Edward Steichen. The center petals are blue, the flowers grow to a diameter of 2½ to 3 inches with spikes 3½ to 4 feet in blossom at one time.

Carl Sandburg with his wife and children care for their large herd of goats and kids at Chikaming Farm in Michigan. At the left, Sandburg holds a Nubian kid, as a Toggenburg looks on.

"*Who shall speak for the people?*
who has the answers?
where is the sure interpreter?
who knows what to say?"

THE PEOPLE, YES

Carl Sandburg and Edward Steichen

"Brothers-in-law who became brothers"

"*To know silence perfectly is to know music.*"
GOOD MORNING, AMERICA

*"I was born on the prairie and the milk of its wheat, the red of its clover,
the eyes of its women, gave me a song and a slogan."*

CORNHUSKERS

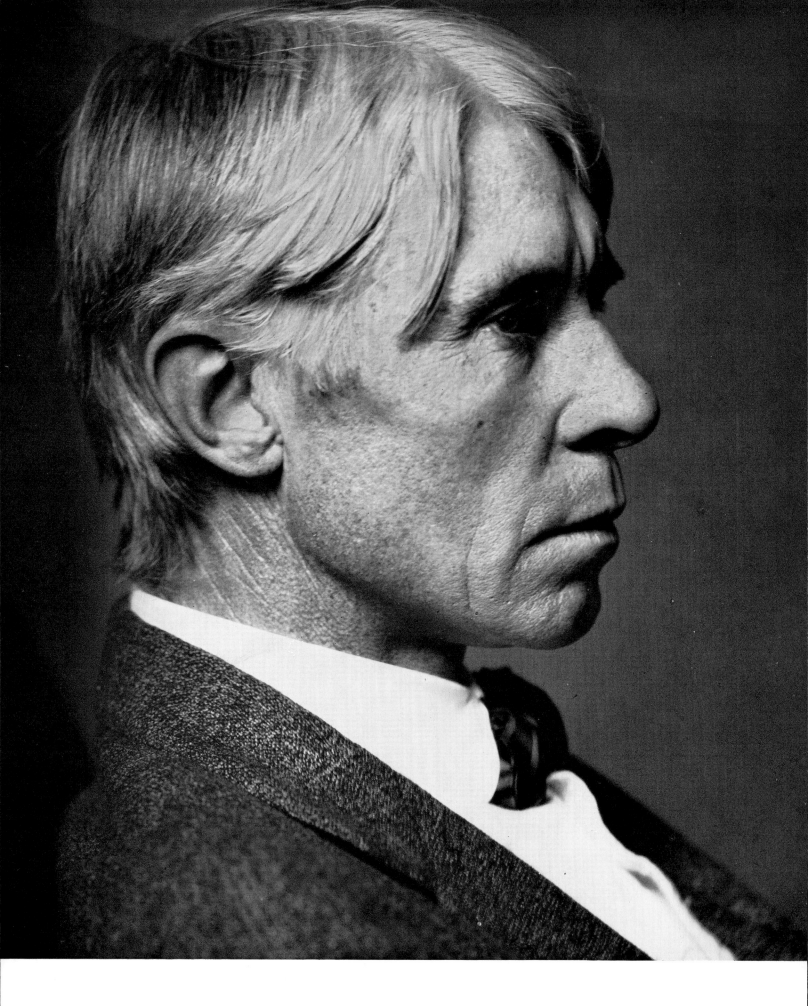

Sculptor Jo Davidson models a head of Sandburg in his Manhattan studio.

"Poetry is a fossil rock-print of a fin and a wing, with an illegible oath between."

GOOD MORNING, AMERICA

Carl Sandburg with Fingal, Edward Steichen's first Irish wolfhound, at the Steichen home, Umpawaug, Connecticut

Lake Michigan Shore

"Hoarfrost and silence:
  Only the muffling
  Of winds dark and lonesome—
  Great lullabies to the long sleepers."

CORNHUSKERS

"Sell me dried wood that has ached with passion clutching the knees and arms of a storm . . .
Sell me something crushed in the heartsblood of pain readier than ever for one more song."

CORNHUSKERS

"*There is a way the moon looks into the timber at night*
  And tells the walnut trees secrets of silver sand—"

GOOD MORNING, AMERICA

Where the Sandburgs planted young poplars to hold the sand between the pine trees
at the house in Michigan, a forest now stands.

Alfred Harcourt was a young book salesman for Henry Holt & Co., selling books in the Middle West, when he first heard about a young poet named Carl Sandburg whose work had appeared in POETRY MAGAZINE, edited by Harriet Monroe. In 1914, Miss Monroe's assistant, Alice Corbin, came to New York with a manuscript by Sandburg called CHICAGO POEMS. Harcourt immediately recognized its value, and after some difficulty persuaded the rather conservative management to publish these bold new works in 1916, followed by a second volume, CORNHUSKERS, in 1918. Harcourt left Holt in 1919 to establish his own firm, and in 1920 he published Sandburg's third book, SMOKE AND STEEL. This picture was taken in Alfred Harcourt's office on the publication of ABRAHAM LINCOLN: THE WAR YEARS, in 1939, for which Sandburg won the Pulitzer Prize.

"*For a number of years I have gone hither and yon over the United States meeting audiences to whom I talked about poetry and art, read my verses, and closed a program with half or quarter hour of songs, giving verbal footnotes with each song. These itineraries have now included about two-thirds of the state universities of the country, audiences ranging from 3,000 people at the University of California to 30 at the Garret Club in Buffalo, New York, and organizations as diverse as the Poetry Society of South Carolina and the Knife and Fork Club of South Bend.*"

THE AMERICAN SONGBAG

(Above) In Michigan, Carl Sandburg worked on a rooftop deck, designed to accommodate sunlight, privacy, and coffee.

(Opposite) Indoors in Michigan, his office was the huge attic, where he worked surrounded by his books, music, and vast archives packed in orange crates.

Four generations

Carl Sandburg with his daughter Helga and her children,
Paula and John Carl; at Birchwood Beach in Michigan
with John Carl; with his mother; (opposite, top) with John
Carl in Michigan, 1945; (opposite, bottom) reading aloud
to Paula and John Carl

*"I can remember my father saying, 'Nu ska
vi spela' (Now shall we play). . . . And
the mother . . . five feet five inches in height
. . . tireless muscles on her bones, tireless
about her housework. She did the cooking,
washing, sewing, bedmaking, and house-
cleaning for the family of nine persons."*

ALWAYS THE YOUNG STRANGERS

"A father sees a son nearing manhood.
 What shall he tell that son?
 'Life is hard; be steel; be a rock.'
 And this might stand him for the storms
 and serve him for humdrum and monotony
 and guide him amid sudden betrayals
 and tighten him for slack moments.
 'Life is a soft loam; be gentle; go easy.' "

THE PEOPLE, YES

At Flat Rock, North Carolina, with Roddy Knoop, Jr., and
(opposite) John Carl

"For him the sun was a sign, a symbol.
   He bowed in prayer to what was behind the sun.
   He made songs and dances to the makers and movers
      of the sun."

HONEY AND SALT

(Right) *"Wherever Carl Sandburg goes, at home or abroad, he can't see a chair without picking it up."*

(Below) Carl Sandburg with the late Dana Steichen at Umpawaug Farm in Connecticut

(Above) Carl Sandburg dined with Crown Prince Gustav Adolf of Sweden when the future King stopped in Chicago during a tour of the United States in 1927.

(Below) During the writing of the Lincoln books, Sandburg had many conferences with Oliver R. Barrett, the famous Lincoln collector, and later wrote his biography.

"*Man's life? A candle in the wind, hoar-frost
on stone.
Nothing more certain than death and nothing
more uncertain than the hour.
Men live like birds together in a wood; when
the time comes each takes his flight.
As wave follows wave, so new men take old
men's places.*"

THE PEOPLE, YES

Flat Rock, North Carolina

"Lincoln? was he a poet?
  and did he write verses?
 'I have not willingly planted a thorn
  in any man's bosom.'
 'I shall do nothing through malice; what
  I deal with is too vast for malice.' "

THE PEOPLE, YES

Late afternoon at Connemara Farm

"Sleep is the gift of many spiders
  The webs tie down the sleepers easy."

COMPLETE POEMS

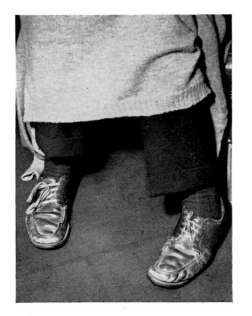

"*Then at last to Springfield came the coffin that had traveled seventeen hundred miles, that had been seen by more than seven million people—and the rigid face on which more than one million five hundred thousand people had gazed a moment or longer. . . .*"

ABRAHAM LINCOLN: THE WAR YEARS

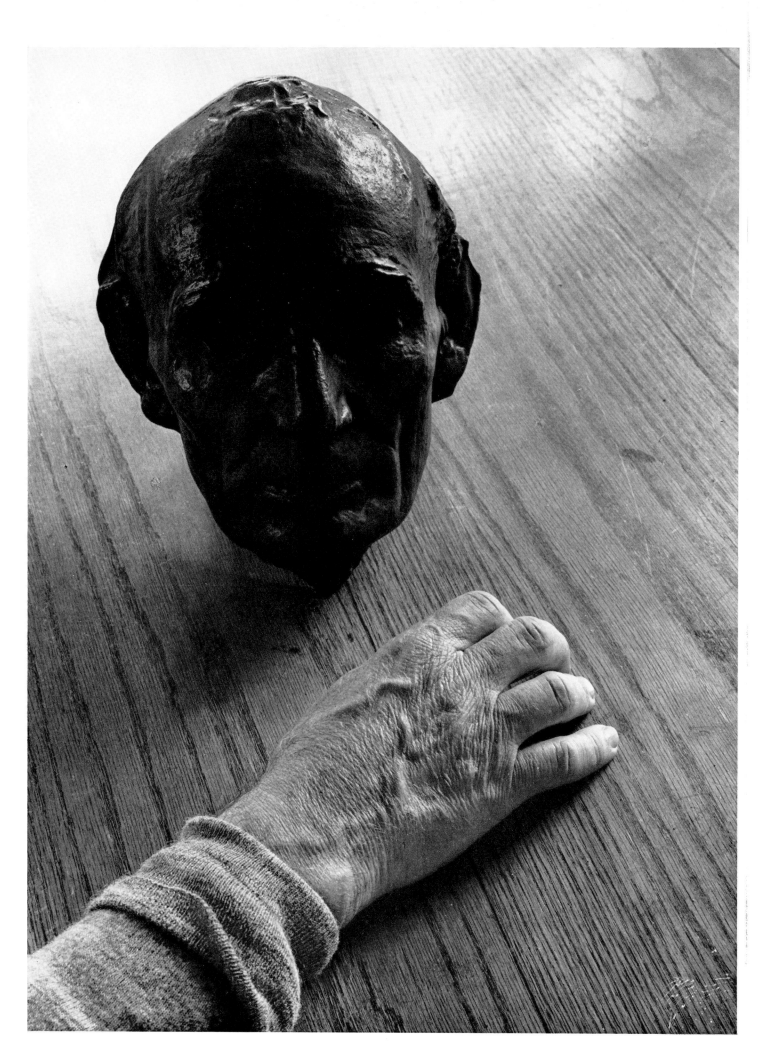

"*Carl Sandburg, like all of the other American poets who came into prominence with him, brought something back to poetry that had been sadly missing in the early years of this century. It was humor, the indispensable ingredient of art as it is of life. . . . Humor is the final sign and seal of seriousness, for it is a proof that reality is held in honor and in love.*"

Mark Van Doren, Introduction to HARVEST POEMS

Chicago

"Hog Butcher for the World,
Tool Maker, Stacker of Wheat,
Player with Railroads and the Nation's Freight Handler;
Stormy, husky, brawling,
City of the Big Shoulders:"

CHICAGO POEMS

(Opposite) When Carl Sandburg appeared at the dedication of The Assembly Hall at the University of Illinois on May 3, 1963, he read Lincoln's farewell speech on leaving Springfield.

Poets Carl Sandburg and Robert Frost with Librarian of Congress L. Quincy Mumford (center) in Washington in 1960. Sandburg was in Washington to receive the silver laurel wreath of the U.S. Chamber of Commerce that night.

Carl Sandburg talks to his publisher, William Jovanovich, President of Harcourt, Brace & World, at his 75th birthday party in Chicago.

(Top) As Eleanor Roosevelt looks on, Sandburg receives a medal from Louis H. Boyar, national chairman of State of Israel Bonds, at the Los Angeles State of Israel Commendation Bond Dinner.

(Bottom) Soviet Ambassador Mikhail Menshikov with his fellow first-nighters Carl Sandburg and Adlai Stevenson at the Chicago Opera House performance of the Moiseyev folk dancers in 1958

Carl Sandburg's 75th birthday parties at his birthplace, Galesburg, Illinois, and in Chicago were attended by 2,000 friends and admirers.

Ambassador Eric Boheman makes Sandburg a Commander in the Order of the North Star.

(Left) He cuts the cake as Mrs. Sandburg and Swedish Ambassador Boheman look on.

(Right, bottom) He chats with Edward Steichen and Fanny Butcher, Chicago book reviewer.

The address of Carl Sandburg before a joint session of Congress, February 12, 1959

Not often in the story of mankind does a man arrive on earth who is both steel and velvet, who is as hard as rock and soft as drifting fog, who holds in his heart and mind the paradox of terrible storm and peace unspeakable and perfect. Here and there across centuries come reports of men alleged to have these contrasts. And the incomparable Abraham Lincoln, born one hundred and fifty years ago this day, is an approach if not a perfect realization of this character.

In the time of the April lilacs in the year 1865, on his death, the casket with his body was carried north and west a thousand miles; and the American people wept as never before; bells sobbed, cities wore crepe; people stood in tears and with hats off as the railroad burial car paused in the leading cities of seven states, ending its journey at Springfield, Illinois, the home town.

During the four years he was President, he at times, especially in the first three months, took to himself the powers of a dictator; he commanded the most powerful armies till then assembled in modern warfare; he enforced conscription of soldiers for the first time in American history; under imperative necessity he abolished the right of habeas corpus; he directed politically and spiritually the wild, massive, turbulent forces let loose in civil war.

He argued and pleaded for compensated emancipation of the slaves. The slaves were property; they were on the tax books along with horses and cattle, the valuation of each slave next to his name on the tax assessor's books. Failing to get action on compensated emancipation, as a Chief Executive having war powers he issued the paper by which he declared the slaves to be free under "military necessity." In the end nearly four billion dollars' worth of property was taken away from those who were legal owners of it—property confiscated, wiped out as by fire and turned to ashes, at his instigation and executive direction. Chattel property recognized and lawful for 250 years was expropriated, seized without payment.

In the month the war began, he told his secretary, John Hay, "My policy is to have no policy." Three years later, in a letter to a Kentucky friend made public, he confessed plainly, "I have been controlled by events." His words at Gettysburg were sacred, yet strange with a color of a familiar: ". . . we cannot consecrate, we cannot hallow, this ground. The brave men, living and dead, who struggled here, have consecrated it, far above our poor power to add or detract."

He could have said, "the brave Union men." Did he have a purpose in omitting the word "Union"? Was he keeping himself and his utterance clear of the passion that would not be good to look at when the time came for peace and reconciliation?

Did he mean to leave an implication that there were brave Union men and brave Confederate men, living and dead, who had struggled there? We do not know, of a certainty.

Was he thinking of the Kentucky father whose two sons died in battle, one in Union blue, the other in Confederate gray, the father inscribing on the stone over their double grave, "God knows which was right"? We do not know.

Lincoln's policies, changing from time to time, aimed at saving the Union. In the end his armies won and his nation became a world power immersed in international politics. In August of 1864 he wrote a memorandum that he expected to lose the next November election. Sudden military victory brought the tide his way; the vote was 2,200,000 for him and 1,800,000 against him.

Among his bitter opponents were such figures as Samuel F. B. Morse, inventor of the telegraph, and Cyrus H. McCormick, inventor of the farm reaper. In all its essential propositions, the Southern Confederacy had the moral support of powerful, respectable elements throughout the North, probably more than a million voters believing in the justice of the Southern cause.

While the war winds howled he insisted that the Mississippi was one river meant to belong to one country, that railroad connection from coast to coast must be pushed through and the Union Pacific Railroad made a reality. While the luck of war wavered and broke and came again, as generals failed and campaigns were lost, he held enough forces of the North together to raise new armies and supply them, until generals were found who made war as victorious war has always been made, with terror, frightfulness, destruction, and on both sides, North and South, valor and sacrifice past words of man to tell.

In the mixed shame and blame of the immense wrongs of two crashing civilizations, often with nothing to say, he said nothing, slept not at all, and on occasions he was seen to weep in a way that made weeping appropriate, decent, majestic.

As he rode alone on horseback near Soldiers' Home on the edge of Washington one night, his hat was shot off; a son he loved died as he watched at the bed; his wife was accused of betraying information to the enemy, until denials from him were necessary.

An Indiana man at the White House heard him say, "Voorhees, don't it seem strange to you that I, who could never so much as cut off the head of a chicken, should be elected, or selected, into the midst of all this blood?"

He tried to guide General Nathaniel Prentiss Banks, three times elected Governor of Massachusetts, in the governing of some seventeen of the forty-eight parishes of

Louisiana controlled by the Union armies, an area holding a fourth of the slaves of Louisiana. He would like to see the state recognize the Emancipation Proclamation. "And while she is at it, I think it would not be objectionable for her to adopt some practical system by which the two races could gradually live themselves out of their old relation to each other, and both come out better prepared for the new. Education for young blacks should be included in the plan."

To Governor Michael Hahn, elected in 1864 by a majority of the 11,000 white male voters who had taken the oath of allegiance to the Union, Lincoln wrote:

"Now you are about to have a convention which, among other things, will probably define the elective franchise. I barely suggest for your private consideration, whether some of the colored people may not be let in—as for instance, the very intelligent, and especially those who have fought gallantly in our ranks."

Among the million words in the Lincoln utterance record, he interprets himself with a more keen precision than someone else offering to explain him. His simple opening of the House Divided speech in 1858 serves for today:

"If we could first know *where* we are, and *whither* we are tending, we could better judge *what* to do, and *how* to do it."

To his Kentucky friend Joshua F. Speed, he wrote in 1855:

"Our progress in degeneracy appears to me to be pretty rapid. As a nation, we began by declaring 'all men are created equal.' We now practically read it 'all men are created equal, *except negroes.*' When the Know-Nothings get control, it will read 'all men are created equal, except negroes, *and foreigners, and catholics.*' When it comes to this I should prefer emigrating to some country where they make no pretense of loving liberty. . . ."

Infinitely tender was his word from a White House balcony to a crowd on the White House lawn, "I have not willingly planted a thorn in any man's bosom," or to a military governor, "I shall do nothing through malice; what I deal with is too vast for malice."

He wrote for Congress to read on December 1, 1862:

"In times like the present, men should utter nothing for which they would not willingly be responsible through time and in eternity."

Like an ancient psalmist he warned Congress:

"Fellow citizens, *we* cannot escape history. We . . . will be remembered in spite of ourselves. No personal significance or insignificance can spare one or another of us. The fiery trial through which we pass will light us down, in honor or dishonor, to the latest generation."

Wanting Congress to break and forget past traditions his words came keen and flashing: "The dogmas of the quiet past are inadequate to the stormy present . . . we must think anew, and act anew. We must disenthrall ourselves." They are the sort of words that actuated the mind and will of the men who created and navigated that marvel of the sea, the Nautilus, on her voyage from Pearl Harbor and under the North Pole icecap.

The people of many other countries take Lincoln now for their own. He belongs to them. He stands for decency, honest dealing, plain talk, and funny stories. "Look where he came from—don't he know all us strugglers and wasn't he a kind of tough struggler all his life right up to the finish?" Something like that you can hear in any nearby neighborhood and across the seas.

Millions there are who take him as a personal treasure. He had something they would like to see spread everywhere over the world. Democracy? We can't find words to say exactly what it is, but he had it. In his blood and bones he carried it. In the breath of his speeches and writings it is there. Popular government? Republican institutions? Government where the people have the say-so, one way or another telling their elected leaders what they want? He had the idea. It's there in the lights and shadows of his personality, a mystery that can be lived but never fully spoken in words.

Our good friend the poet and playwright Mark Van Doren tells us:

"To me, Lincoln seems, in some ways, the most interesting man who ever lived. He was gentle, but his gentleness was combined with a terrific toughness, an iron strength."

How did Lincoln say he would like to be remembered? His beloved friend Representative Owen Lovejoy, of Illinois, had died in May of 1864 and friends wrote to Lincoln and he replied that the pressure of duties kept him from joining them in efforts for a marble monument to Lovejoy, the last sentence of his letter saying, "Let him have the marble monument along with the well-assured and more enduring one in the hearts of those who love liberty unselfishly for all men."

So perhaps we may say that the well-assured and most enduring memorial to Lincoln is invisibly there, today, tomorrow and for a long time yet to come. It is there in the hearts of lovers of liberty, men and women who understand that wherever there is freedom there have been those who fought, toiled and sacrificed for it.

Carl Sandburg speaking in Washington at the 100th anniversary of Lincoln's inauguration

(From left to right, flanking Sandburg) House Speaker Sam Rayburn, Representative Fred Schwengel. (Background, left to right) House Doorkeeper William Miller, Senator Carl Hayden, Senator Vance Hartke, Representative Peter Mack, Representative Charles Halleck, Senator Everett Dirkson.

"*I wanted a man's face looking into the jaws and throat of life*
With something proud on his face, so proud no smash of the jaws,
No gulp of the throat leaves the face in the end
With anything else than the old proud look . . ."

A visit to Gettysburg for a television interview with Howard K. Smith

"To think incessantly of blood and steel, steel and blood, the argument without end by the mouths of brass cannon, of a mystic cause carried aloft and sung on dripping and crimson bayonet points—to think so and thus across nights and months folding up into years, was a wearing and a grinding that brought questions. What is this teaching and who learns from it and where does it lead?"

ABRAHAM LINCOLN: THE WAR YEARS

Edward Steichen watches as Carl Sandburg types his preface for the monumental exhibition and book THE FAMILY OF MAN.

"The Family of Man" exhibition travels to Russia, accompanied by Sandburg and Steichen.
Here Sandburg stands next to Steichen's photograph of Lincoln's life mask.

(Top) Departure for Russia to witness the opening of
"The Family of Man" exhibition

(Bottom) Singing for Russian writers at the Moscow Literary Union

Arriving in Sweden after a good-will trip to Moscow for the United States Information Agency, Sandburg and Steichen are welcomed by Mrs. Caroline Hammarskiold, her husband, photographer Hans Hammarskiold, and their children.

Sweden: (Top) Among the other rewards of the trip to the homeland was the gold medal Sandburg received from King Gustav Adolf, and his 28th honorary degree—this one from Uppsala University.

(Bottom) Prime Minister Tage Erlander greets Edward Steichen and Carl Sandburg at Harpsund, the official residence of the Prime Minister of Sweden, outside Stockholm.

"*My father . . . had never learned to write. When his father and mother died in Sweden his schooling had only taught him to read and he earned some kind of a living as a chore boy in a distillery. He became a teamster at the distillery, finally laying by enough money to buy steerage passage to America, to 'the new country where there was a better chance.'*"

ALWAYS THE YOUNG STRANGERS

Sweden: Visiting his parents' birthplace

"Memory is when you look back
and the answers float in
to who? what? when? where?

The members who were there then
are repeated on a screen
are recalled on a scroll
are moved in a miniature drama,
are collected and recollected
for actions, speeches, silences,
set forth by images of the mind
and made in a mingling mist
to do again and to do over
precisely what they did do once—
this is memory—
sometimes slurred and blurred—
this is remembering—
sometimes wrecking the images
and proceeding again to reconstruct
what happened and how,
the many little involved answers
to who? what? when? where?
and more involved than any
    how? how?"

COMPLETE POEMS

Sandburg had visited Sweden as a young reporter in 1918, but in 1959, with Steichen, he had his first real opportunity to see the country of his ancestors, and the farms in Appuna and Åsbo, where his mother and father were raised.

One of the highlights of Sandburg's trip to Sweden was his participation in the annual Swedish-American day ceremonies at Skansen, the national park in Stockholm. He talked, read from his poems, sang, and generally cheered and charmed his kinsmen.

"A biography, sirs, should begin—with the breath of a man when his eyes first meet the light of day—then working on through to the death when the light of day is gone."

HONEY AND SALT

Paula, Helga, and Carl Sandburg examine a few of the awards he has received during the past half-century.

(Opposite) Carl Sandburg and Edward Steichen in Moscow

(Top) Sandburg and Steichen in Paris
(Bottom) David Douglas Duncan, Edward Steichen, and Carl Sandburg in Paris

At a party in New York, Carl Sandburg and Edward Steichen are introduced to Johanna Taub, who a short time later became Mrs. Edward Steichen.

Sandburg has been an actor as well as a poet—not as a performer, but as a keen participant in the media of communications. Above left, he appears with Ed Sullivan on his television program; right, with Milton Berle; below, he discusses a speech with newspaper publisher Ralph McGill. Right, he meets some of the cast of "The Greatest Story Ever Told," a motion picture: left to right, Van Heflin, Ed Wynn, and Joseph Schildkraut.

Music has always been an essential ingredient of Sandburg's life. He has performed with André Kostelanetz, the conductor (top); Segovia (center) gave him tips on playing the guitar; and he spent many evenings singing and playing with his old friend Lloyd Lewis, noted Chicago writer and Lincoln scholar.

Frank Lloyd Wright and Carl Sandburg shared many mutual interests, ranging from architecture to poetry. "Frank was an ideal companion. We had a fine time together."

On a trip to New York he renewed his acquaintance with Marilyn Monroe, whom he had previously met in Hollywood. She taught him some new dance steps; he demonstrated exercises that might help her insomnia. *"She was very good company . . . she had a genuine quality, and a mind out of the ordinary for show people. I gave her a book of my complete poetry. I wanted her to have it. . . . She had some faith in me."*

Visitors come to Connemara Farm from all over the world. Among them were Edward R. Murrow (below), who fashioned a memorable television interview from his meeting with Sandburg, and George T. Stevens (opposite), who consulted him on the screenplay for "The Greatest Story Ever Told."

97

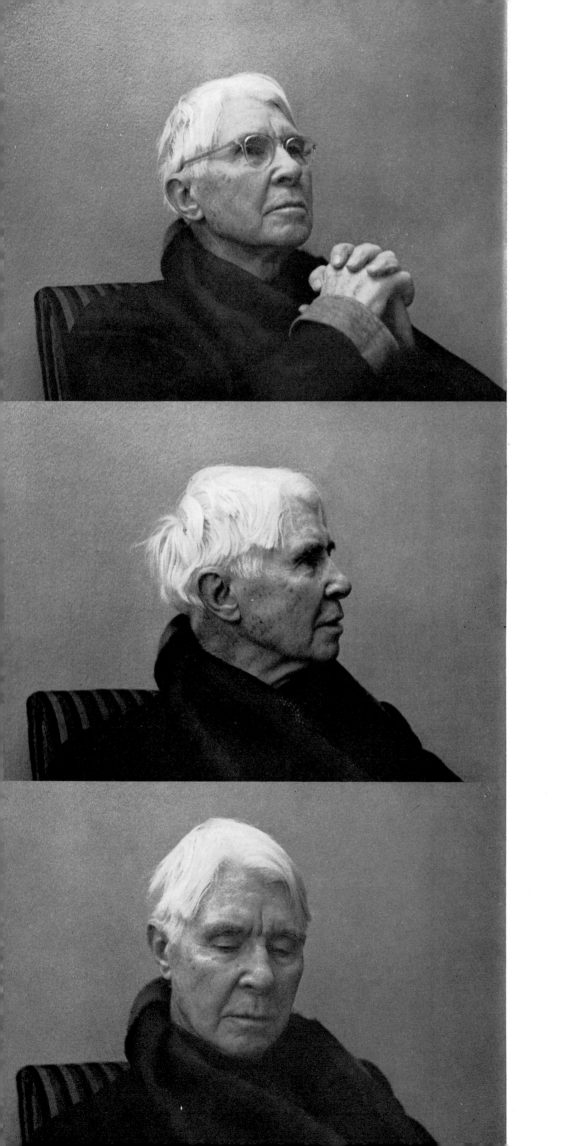

After a visit with President John F. Kennedy, in October 1961, Sandburg said: *"The way he's going is almost too good to be true. There was never a more formidable situation of historical conditions for a Chief Executive to face. It is not quite as serious as Lincoln's. But time may prove that after all it is nearly as dark as when Lincoln took over."*

"*Over the years Carl Sandburg has manifested certain habits which in another person could be described as affectations. He had a period when he always covered his knees with a blanket or shawl whenever he sat down. During another phase, he would always wear a scarf around his neck. Obviously this was not a response to temperature, since he would wear blanket, shawl, or scarf in both summer and winter.*"

On April 20, 1964, the Sandburgs and the Steichens visited President and Mrs. Lyndon B. Johnson in Washington for a tour of the White House. The President had extended the invitation on January 6, when he telephoned Sandburg to wish him a happy 86th birthday. At that time he told Sandburg that he hoped that when he reached the poet's age, he would have done "half as much for the country as Sandburg has done." Mr. Sandburg said it was the first time he had received a call from a President since he was a reporter for the Chicago DAILY NEWS.

A demonstration of a typical Sandburg gesture—how to hold a cigar butt

"He still cuts every cigar in half and he smokes each part to the bitter end. When he can no longer hold it he fixes it on the tip of his pocket knife. Whether because he enjoys the hot taste of the smoke or whether it is just another reflection of early days and not to waste anything no one knows, not even Carl."

Connemara Farm—goats, gardens, and peace
"When will man know what birds know?"

Mr. and Mrs. Carl Sandburg stand on the porch of their house at Flat Rock, North Carolina.

*"What I need mainly is three things in life, possibly four.
To be out of jail, to eat regular, to get what I write printed,
and a little love at home and a little outside."*

The Sandburg home in North Carolina was built in 1838; it looks out over sweeping valleys to the Appalachians and the Blue Ridge Mountains.

(Top left) Dinner with the Knoop family; (lower left) a joke with Harry Golden; (below) a song for Paula

"How much do you love me, a million bushels?
  Oh, a lot more than that, Oh, a lot more."
                    SMOKE AND STEEL

At Connemara

"*Nothing else in this song—only your face.*
Nothing else here—only your drinking, night-gray eyes."
SMOKE AND STEEL